MARTIAL ARTS

JUDO

BY HEATHER ROOK BYLENGA

WWW.APEXEDITIONS.COM

Apex is distributed by North Star Editions:
sales@northstareditions.com | 888-417-0195

Produced for Apex by Red Line Editorial.

Photographs ©: David Svab/CTK/AP Images, cover; Shutterstock Images, 1, 10–11, 12, 13, 14–15, 16–17, 18, 19, 20, 21, 22–23, 24–25, 26–27, 29; iStockphoto, 4–5, 6–7, 8–9

Library of Congress Control Number: 2023910171

ISBN
978-1-63738-764-1 (hardcover)
978-1-63738-807-5 (paperback)
978-1-63738-889-1 (ebook pdf)
978-1-63738-850-1 (hosted ebook)

Printed in the United States of America
Mankato, MN
012024

NOTE TO PARENTS AND EDUCATORS

Apex books are designed to build literacy skills in striving readers. Exciting, high-interest content attracts and holds readers' attention. The text is carefully leveled to allow students to achieve success quickly. Additional features, such as bolded glossary words for difficult terms, help build comprehension.

TABLE OF CONTENTS

CHAPTER 1

THROWS AND HOLDS

A girl steps onto a mat. It's her first judo competition. The girl and her **opponent** bow to each other. Then the **referee** starts the match.

In judo matches, both fighters start out standing.

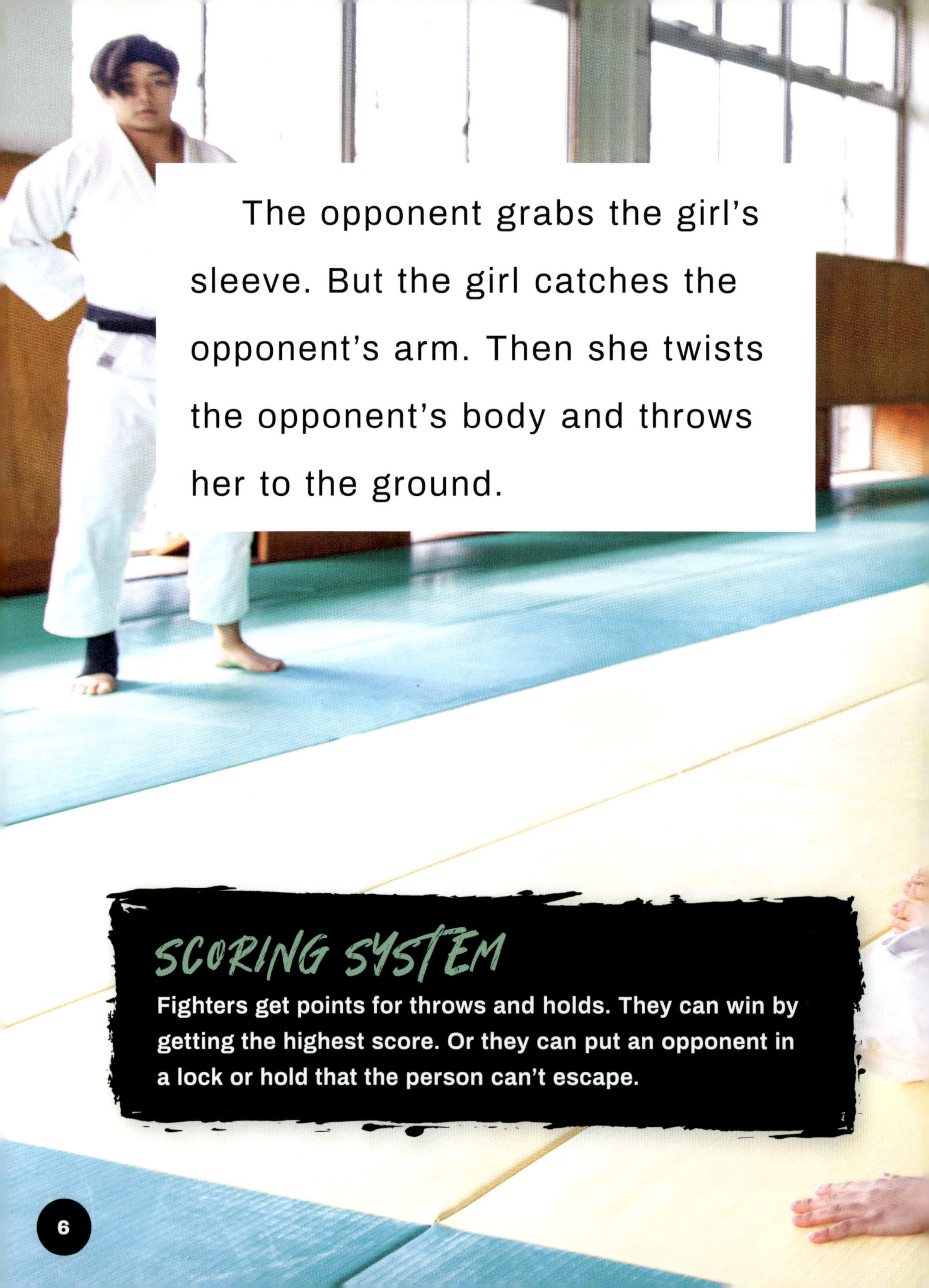

The opponent grabs the girl's sleeve. But the girl catches the opponent's arm. Then she twists the opponent's body and throws her to the ground.

SCORING SYSTEM

Fighters get points for throws and holds. They can win by getting the highest score. Or they can put an opponent in a lock or hold that the person can't escape.

Many judo moves involve grabbing an opponent's clothing.

The opponent lands on her side. The girl pins her down. The opponent can't get away. So, the girl wins.

FAST FACT

Most judo matches last four to five minutes.

Fighters try to pin one another to the mat.

CHAPTER 2

HISTORY OF JUDO

Judo comes from Japan. Jigoro Kano created it. Kano studied jiu-jitsu. That fighting style had been used by **samurai**. They used it for battle.

Jigoro Kano lived from 1860 to 1938.

Kano's judo school was located at Eisho-ji Temple.

In 1882, Kano started his own **martial arts** school. Kano took out jiu-jitsu's hits and kicks. He added throws and holds. He called this new style judo.

A SOFTER STYLE

Judo means "gentle way" in Japanese. Kano designed it to help people exercise and defend themselves. Over time, though, judo's rules changed. It became more competitive.

The moves used at judo events can be similar to wrestling.

By the 1960s, judo had spread around the world. People began holding international competitions. Today, millions of people enjoy watching and practicing judo.

FAST FACT

Men's judo was first part of the Olympics in 1964. Women's judo was added in 1992.

People from 82 countries competed at the Paris Grand Slam in 2023.

CHAPTER 3

LEARNING JUDO

Judo focuses on **self-defense**. It teaches ways to turn an opponent's movements against them.

Judo fighters practice keeping their balance while twisting or throwing opponents.

Judo students are called judokas. They attend schools called dojos. There, students train and **spar** with one another.

A judo teacher is called a sensei.

Judo belts go through several colors. The highest ranks use black and red.

JUDOGIS

Judokas wear uniforms called judogis. A judogi has a jacket, pants, and a belt. The belt's color shows the student's **rank**. Students start with white belts. They get new colors as they build skills.

Choke holds wrap around a person's neck. These moves are dangerous. So, only high-level fighters do them.

Students learn ways to knock opponents down. They also practice locks and holds. These moves trap opponents. Fighters wrap arms or legs around their opponent's body.

FAST FACT

Judokas practice ways to fall safely. These moves are called breakfalls.

Some breakfalls use rolls. They help people avoid hurting their heads or necks.

CHAPTER 4

COMPETITIONS

Many judokas compete. They go to events and **tournaments**. Fighters are split into categories. These groups are often based on weight.

At events, fighters may be grouped based on age, gender, size, and skill.

If neither fighter submits, the one with the highest score wins.

Then, judokas fight one-on-one. Each match takes place on a large mat. Fighters score points for how well they do throws and holds. They also try to get opponents to submit, or give up.

SUBMITTING

To give up, fighters can say *maitta*. That means "I submit" in Japanese. Or they can slap the mat twice. This is called tapping out.

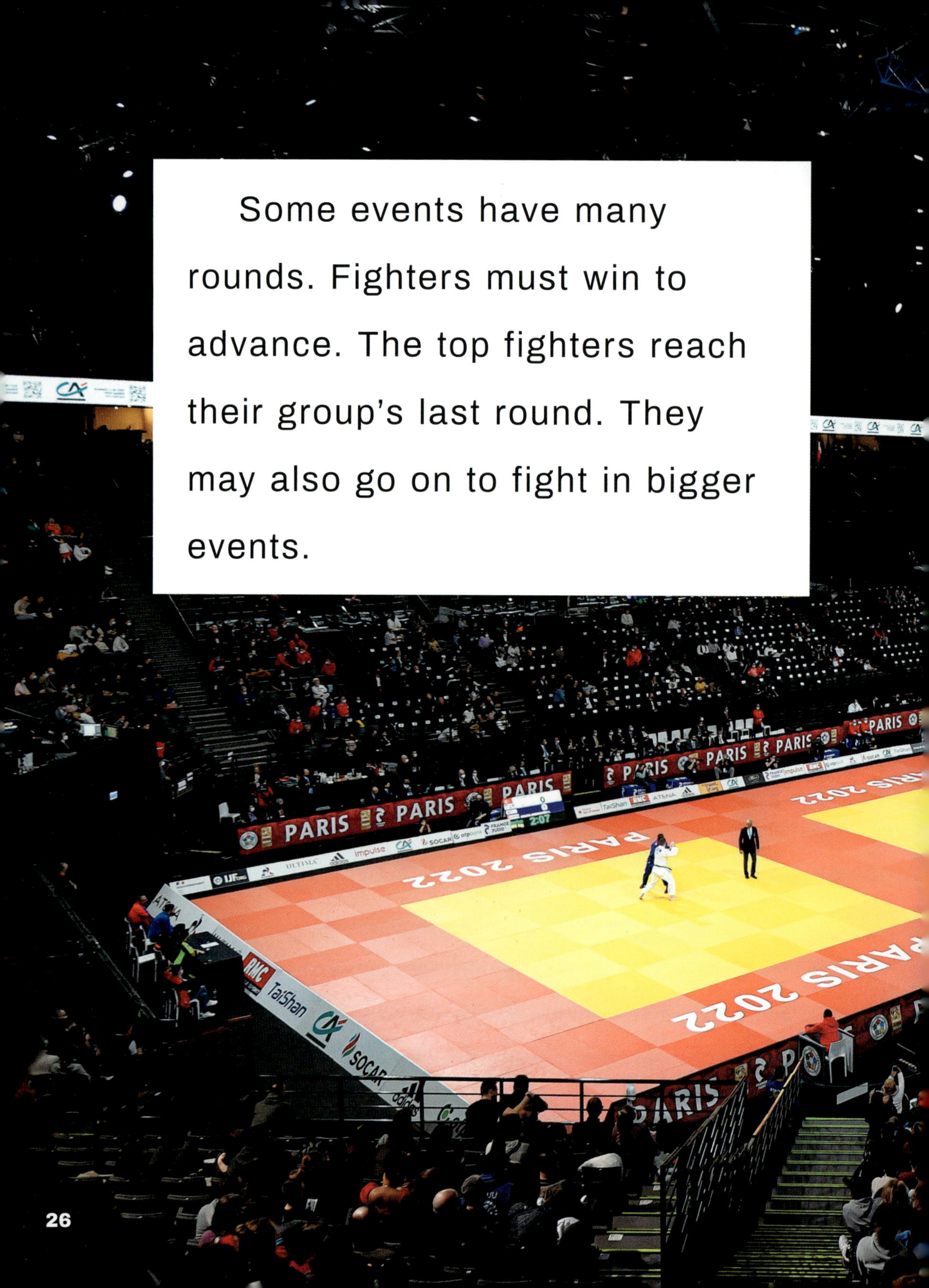

Some events have many rounds. Fighters must win to advance. The top fighters reach their group's last round. They may also go on to fight in bigger events.

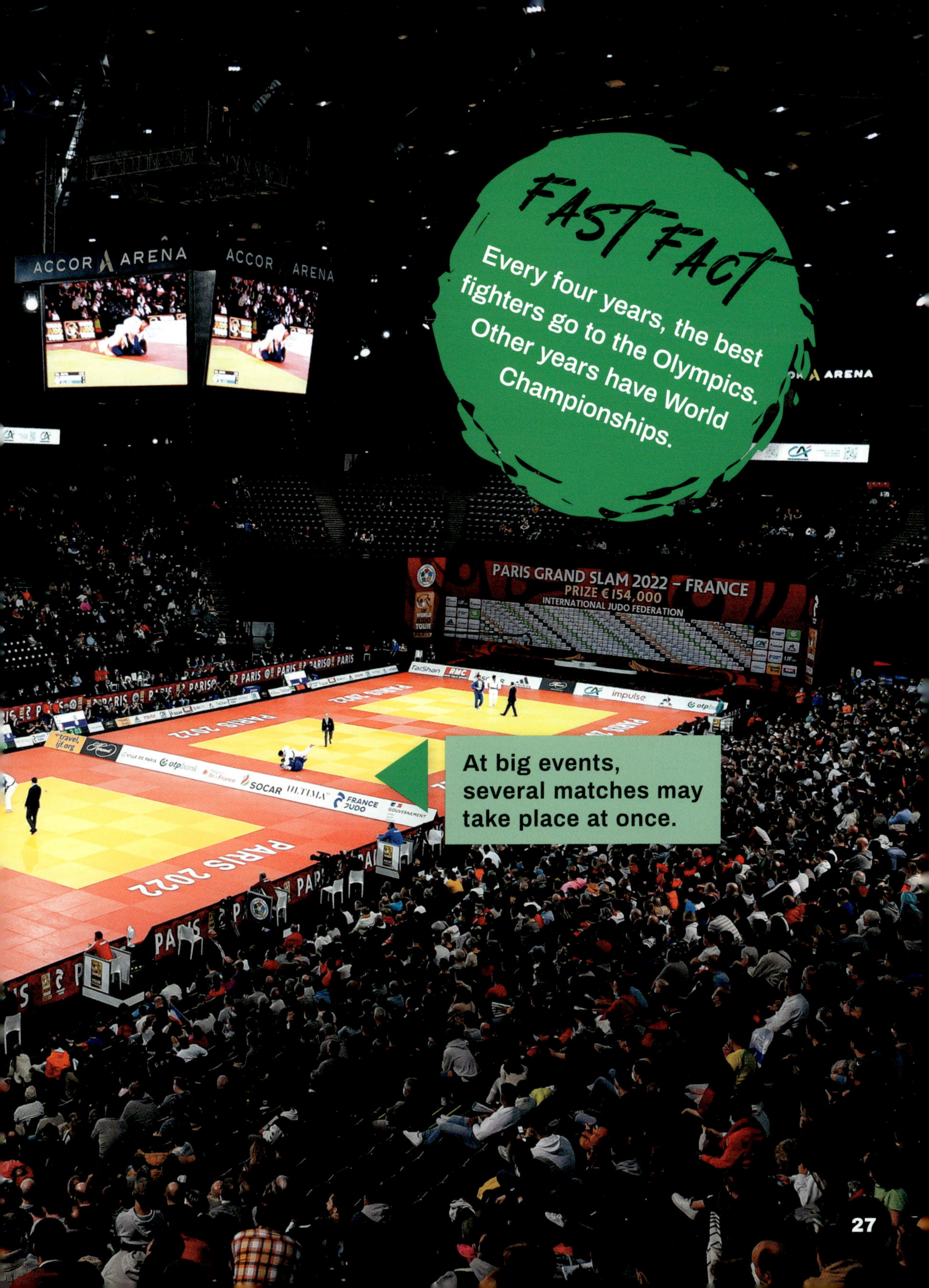

FAST FACT

Every four years, the best fighters go to the Olympics. Other years have World Championships.

At big events, several matches may take place at once.

COMPREHENSION QUESTIONS

Write your answers on a separate piece of paper.

1. Write a few sentences explaining the ways people score points in judo matches.

2. Would you like to take judo classes at a dojo? Why or why not?

3. When did Jigoro Kano start his judo school?

A. 1882
B. 1964
C. 1992

4. When did judo first become part of the Olympics?

A. 1882
B. 1964
C. 1992

5. What does **international** mean in this book?

*By the 1960s, judo had spread around the world. People began holding **international** competitions.*

A. involving many countries
B. involving just one country
C. involving just one person

6. What does **focuses** mean in this book?

*Judo **focuses** on self-defense. It teaches ways to turn an opponent's movements against them.*

A. shines light
B. puts attention
C. leaves out

Answer key on page 32.

GLOSSARY

martial arts

Skills used for fighting or self-defense, such as karate or tae kwon do.

opponent

A person who someone is fighting against.

rank

A level of skill or ability.

referee

A person who makes sure rules are followed.

samurai

Warriors who fought in Japan from the late 1100s to the 1800s.

self-defense

Ways to fight back or stay safe if attacked.

spar

To fight with another person as a sport or for practice.

tournaments

Events where people try to win several matches or rounds.

TO LEARN MORE

BOOKS

Corso, Phil. *Jujitsu*. New York: PowerKids Press, 2020.

Price, Karen. *GOATs of Olympic Sports*. Minneapolis: Abdo Publishing, 2022.

Roza, Greg. *Judo*. New York: PowerKids Press, 2020.

ONLINE RESOURCES

Visit **www.apexeditions.com** to find links and resources related to this title.

ABOUT THE AUTHOR

Heather Rook Bylenga lives in the Pacific Northwest with her family. Outdoors, she can be found hiking or running. Indoors, she can be found curled up on her couch with a book and a cup of tea.

INDEX

ANSWER KEY:
1. Answers will vary; 2. Answers will vary; 3. A; 4. B; 5. A; 6. B